Dyn

Get Off Your Ass And Cold Call

"Humorous, inspiring, a rejuvenation to those who carry dreams and those who dare to dream of making a difference in life and career. Get Off Your Ass And Cold Call is a journey through the life of a man who has maintained stamina and resilience on and off the field. It is a leap into the choices we are faced with, to do or die or to live and learn while embarking on our own individual spiritual path to success."

-Dionne Character, Author

CoverPhoto by Gregory Prescott

Manufactured in the United States of America

ISBN: 978-1-7346383-1-8

Publisher/Author contact: dynast@dynastamir.com

For information regarding discounts or bulk purchases, please email.

Dynast Amir

Amir draws from his outrageous life experiences,

making this body of work "one hell of a read."

\-   Ramone Boddie

Get Off Your Ass And Cold Call

ACKNOWLEDGEMENTS

I would like to thank God and the ancestors for the experiences that inspired me to write this book. Ramone, for staying on me to accomplish something worthwhile outside of my corporate career. And of course, my family, mom and dad and everyone that I have come in contact with during this 30-year journey that has helped to mold me into the man that I am today.
Thank You.

"You must utilize all of your mental abilities to accomplish your goals, and when you are disappointed, you must use all of your magnetic will power to get what you want."

CONTENTS

FOREWORD

When DM's,decision-makers, and or potential clients first see him; they are quick to notice his radiant aura and dynamic charm. His smooth good looks and athletic swag always wins them over. Turning his most stubborn decision-makers into very grateful clients, plain and simple, Dynast Amir is a super successful sales rep with a paradoxical beginning which means, he is somewhat humble yet at the same time has a cocky demeanor.

"You must utilize all of your mental abilities to accomplish your goals, and when you are disappointed, you must use all of your magnetic will power to get what you want." This axiom is affirmed daily by Mr. Dynast Amir whom before at an earlier time in his life was an All-American track and football athlete at Christian Brothers High School in Sacramento, California. A graduate of the University of Georgia, given his status as a sought-after jock and one heck of a ladies man, it's no wonder Mr. Amir draws from his outrageous life experiences, which makes this body of work *Get Off Your Ass And Cold Call*" one hell of a read. It's not just another corny sales book but a mental adventure. I could not help but laugh throughout the entire proofread. I have watched Mr. Dynast Amir grow from scraping up change just to eat a pack of top ramen to joining the elite 10% of income earners in America. The book is a sure winner of true inspiration and hallmarks, an instant hit with all average salespeople who aspire to be the best that they can be.

Join me in the journey of Dynast Amir's tale as he tells all revealing the secrets to his amazing quest of success through spirituality, life jewels, and plain ole common sense. How did this self-criticizing, self-proclaimed underachieving African American male make his way to such a decadent place in the corporate arena?

Ramone Boddie
Mentor

INTRODUCTION

*"When shit hits the fan, entertainment,
prostitution and sales will all survive the economic downfall."*

I was told this a few years back by a close elder of mine. When people are stressed over money, entertainment – i.e., movies, dancing and drinking – is a temporary outlet to remove the thoughts of not having two dimes in your pocket to rub together. Prostitution goes hand-in-hand with entertainment,for it is also considered the oldest profession in the world. I have to disagree. For sex is a great outlet to distract you from money woes, but sales IMHO is the oldest profession on the planet. Why? The prostitute has to first convince or sell the potential John on why he/she should pay a fee for his/her sexual services. With that being said, you have to sell yourself before you can actually be considered a prostitute.

The economy experienced a sizable dip in 2006. The shit was about to hit the fan. Porn/prostitution was not an option. I could not look my mother in the face after performing in a threesome with Janet Jacme and Heather Hunter on camera. She would disown me. I could not envision myself being a sales guy at the time.So me personally, with my black Ken doll looks and Batman action-figure six-pack, I gave entertainment a shot to no avail. I have little patience for the ego-driven looser who usually works the check-in at casting calls. So the last option, even though I ran from it on the onset, was sales.

I am a sales guy, the Jehovah Witnesses of the professional world. Yes, I'm that guy that totally ignores the "no solicitation" sign on your door, the guy that totally shows up to your business unannounced at any time of the day. I can be annoying as hell to some people, but it's annoyance with grace and class. Many people are ignorant about what we do and how we are paid. We also are the Rodney Dangerfields of corporate America. "We barely get any respect, especially from that bougie 'Hollywood' aspiring actor/actress crew whom you can find during the week or weekends waiting tables at Toast, for you walk in and they are utterly standoffish. They act like they run the restaurant and are very impolite to the point where all you want to say is, "Look, what I can make in a day, you will not make in a month."

Ok guys, I swear I am as humble as can be; I just had to vent. With movies like *Pursuit of Happyness, Death of a Salesman,* and *Glengarry Glen Ross,* the common misconception of salespeople is that we are money-hungry, blood-sucking vampires who are always desperate to make a sale, because we are close to being evicted from our extended stay in the part of town you don't enter between the hours of 8 p.m. to 5 a.m.If you have not seen these movies, please go rent them. The most successful salespeople are compensated very well – and when I say very well, I mean a six-figure income or close to it. Sales afford us the lifestyle that we want to live. We usually make more than the business owners we deal with. We are definitely in the top 10% of income earners in America along with Donald Trump, Ronald M. Popeil, inventor of the chop-o-matic, and those Illuminati guys you know the guys that are responsible for the murder of Tupac and who were also responsible for cancelling *Alf* from our major networks. Yes, "us" salespeople are in good company.

Some loathe cold calling, but I personally welcome it, for I know that it isthe first step in positioning me to accomplish the majority of the materialistic goals that I have set for myself. I embrace cold calling and every sales professional should as well. It's not sexy. Cold calling is not the most glamorous activity in the world.Without cold calling, I would not be a successful salesperson, and this book would not have been written. Embrace and accept cold calling with an open mind and heart, for it is the necessary first step in attaining sales glory and with sales, glory comes one of the benefits of being a prominent sales rep – more cash.

1
CHAPTER
My Secret

What is the secret? It's really no secret. I do what the majority of people don't do. I work my ass off, but I do more than work my ass off. First, I visualize what I want then I implement a strategic plan.I then execute this plan by going after it. No excuses. Why? Because excuses are the talk of the incompetent, and those that choose to use them seldom amount to anything. When I see something I want, I develop a significant case of tunnel vision. Nothing is going to get in my way of accomplishing what I have to achieve and I mean nothing. Negative people that get in my way or say I can't accomplish what I have in front of me, get out of my way along with the other people that want to rain on my parade. If you are not with me but against me, you are merely a distraction that needs to be removed from my surroundings.

The reality of most people is that they are content with being an average Joe or just another guy, content with just having an average life. They complain about their average life and how it's everyone else's fault and not their own. You know who I'm talking about,the person that's doing 80 mph in a 45mph zone and gets caught and uses the typical, "Well, everyone else is doing it" excuse, or the sales professional content with just hitting their number and not getting fired, and when a prospect doesn't buy from them it's always the "bad" economy, or prices are too high, or there aren't enough leads excuses. Well, *Get Off Your Ass And Cold Call!*

Dynast Amir

This book is not only a sales book.It's a book that deals with life. If you ask the majority of salespeople what they least like about their job, it's cold calling, especially in parts of the South and Midwest where during the summer temperatures can reach the 100's with humidity of 90%. But to accomplish what you desire, you have to pay a price. Cold calling also coincides with life, because if you are not satisfied with life, you are going to have to enforce your will by getting out and causing the change that you want to happen. In sales, visualizing what you want and implementing your plan does not necessarily guarantee instant success. Sometimes the leads will run dry and the prospect list will shrink; prospects that you were counting on to contract might renege, but don't feel sorry for yourself. Get out and go door to door and increase your prospect list in order to put yourself in a position to achieve the goal that you have set out for yourself. This mindset transfers over to everyday life. If you are not content with your lifestyle, or you want that new home, that new car, you want to attract that love interest; you are going to have to impose your will and make it happen. Don't be afraid to ask for the help needed in the attainment of your personal goals. Go back to school and get that accreditation/degree to put yourself in the position to be qualified for an upcoming promotion. Also, try to find a more successful, professional group to hang out with, because you become the people that you hang out with the most. Meetup.com is a great resource in creating a more enterprising peer group.

The stories, my personal experiences, and allegories within *Get Off Your Ass And Cold Call,* are here to help fire you up and stir up some emotion in you to motivate you to take the first step to get up get out and do something and change your current existence.If you are not happy with the current state that you are in or even if you are happy with your current state, this will at least fire you up and make you hungry for more. Never be content in life, always satisfy.

2

CHAPTER
All-Time Low

In January 2010, I was at my lowest financially and spiritually. Seniors were not enrolling in my Medicare supplement programs. Insurance sales were drowsy. I could barely rub two nickels together. I was a month late on my rent, and my landlord, a Jamaican version of Danny DeVito from *The Super*, was demanding that I pay up or be evicted. I was two months late on my car note on my 2001 Black Ford Mustang GT with a Steeda body kit on it. I was 27 at the time, grown man status with no more calling home and belly aching to mom and dad to help me come up with the rent. I had to resort to going back to the oldest profession in the world. Again, some say prostitution; I say sales. So, I went on the job hunt.

First was a 100% commission job for a marketing company – well, I'm not sure if they were 100% commission, but I'm going to assume that they were. Tip: If you are in the process of interviewing for a job and they refuse to tell you how much you can expect for your base salary and every time you inquire on how much you can expect to be compensated, they change the subject...run! It's a 100% commission job. Trust me; I've been there done that. They are going to give you the potential of growth and great opportunity B.S., but don't waste your time or your energy. There is nothing wrong with commission-only sales jobs, and my first sales gig was 100% commission only. Usually, the companies that dance around the compensation question, instead of being upfront about wages, are commonly unprofessional.

For when it is time to pay you for your services, you seldom receive what you are owed.

So I show up to the interview with the marketing company. I have a general business conversation with the guy. During the exchange, I inquire on the company comp plan; coincidentally, he refuses to answer. Shortly thereafter, I leave the interview and never received a call back. Also depending on your career path, be wary of looking for a career on Craigslist. They are usually jobs, not careers, and there's a major difference. This can save a lot of your time and energy. Stick with headhunters. They are hungry. If they do not get you placed in a position, they do not get paid.

The second interview was for a cable company that I found on Craigslist. When I arrived at the job interview, I was baffled because I didn't notice a Los Angeles County Probation Department sign on the front door. I swear, not to be judgmental (I'm lying, I'm judging; we all do to an extent), I was interviewing amongst felons and part-time dope dealers. I give my resume to HR. She places it in a stack of resumes. I then interview with the hiring manager and the first question she asks is,"Where is your resume?"I respond, "It was given to HR and that it's in the stack that HR just handed to you that you are shuffling through." She says, "That she cannot locate my resume," in the termite hill of resumes and then responds,"That if I don't have a resume, I can't interview."Since I was strapped for money, to not interview wasn't an option.I politely asked the manager to, "Please look through that stack again," for I knew that it is in there. She still can't place it. I ask a final question, "So you are telling me that my resume was lost during the transition of resumes from the HR office on the third floor to your office on the fourth floor?" The apathetic manager replies, "I guess so, sorry." I leave the office calmly, but inside I was irate. I was just screwed out of an opportunity to earn $15 an hour. I did the math, that's a whopping $600 a week before taxes. I was fired up. I'll be able to pay my car note on my beat-up Mustang GT with the imposter Steeda emblems, pay my rent, and partake in the weekend warrior life – i.e., go to the club, by a T-shirt and maybe a pair of shoes from SportieLa every weekend, see a movie, and that's about it. This is what I now consider an average life. I experienced a sense of loss by not securing the position.

On my way home from the dismal interview, I remembered that when I was in college, I had access to job recruitment agencies that dealt specifically in placing washed-up athletes like myself into sales jobs. Researching these niche-specific head hunters was not difficult. I found a service, placed my resume on their site, and received a call three hours later from a recruiter for the company. I remembered this same company tried to recruit me out of college to be a manager in training. I passed. Selling towels and soap at the time wasn't as sexy as pharmaceutical sales. Since I was going to be peddling toilet paper and not Cialis, there was no way in hell that toilet paper pushing was more lucrative than selling "dope" legally. This ignorance cost me a lot of money out of college. I ended up selling insurance for Aflac, which gave me a lot of experience.

The recruiter and I had an open dialogue about the toilet paper company called Cintas. I told him, "I was familiar with the company." He then begins to tell me that, "I would be in a division that deals with selling FS products." F.S., or Facility Services, is a sexy term for toilet paper, paper towels, bar towels, and toilet seat covers affectionately known as "ass gaskets" – all very unsexy products. He then tells me that my base salary will be $45,000 and that "Reps that hardly work make at least $60,000 to $75,000 a year." I was blown away. $60,000 to me at that time was a lot of money and still is. My next question was, "Could I start today?" Shortly thereafter, I interviewed and was hired a week later.

One lesson that I learned during this whole ordeal was that to experiencesuccess, you have to first experience some type of failure. If you don't taste some type of failure, you cannot truly define and appreciate success.Celebrate your failures, for through them, you are afforded the opportunity to make it right through success. Being rejected by the other two opportunities caused me to cherish even more of my offer letter that was presented to me by my new employer. This job selling toilet paper has definitely changed my life financially, mentally and spiritually. Like some yoga master once said, "Meditating is made a little easier when you have food on your plate and money in your pocket." I went from praying that I'd land a $ 15-hour job to earning six figures a year just by my resume being "misplaced." There's no telling where I would be right now if they actually found my resume. This book probably wouldn't have been written, and I would be residing in my same studio apartment in Koreatown driving the same mustang. Now, if you are content with this lifestyle, this might not be the book for you.

3
CHAPTER
Your Potential

It's possible to double your income in a year, for I am a living example. Just a change in your way of thinking can afford you a raise in income. It is within reach to realize everything that your heart desires. It's called the power of suggestion, which works in accordance with the subconscious mind. Your subconscious mind is the invisible part of the mind, but it controls your life, your well-being, and how others view you. I have a number of affirmations that I say to program my subconscious mind. To some, they might sound corny, but they are highly effective. Once you reap the benefits of utilizing these techniques, you will not regret being a successful cornball. One of them I chant first thing in the morning and before I go to bed is,"I will always have an abundance and a whole lot to spare." Or, simply chant "Wealth,Success." By saturating your subconscious mind with affirmations like these, soon the conscious mind will begin to act with the information, and positive results will be obtained.

Your friends might think that you are crazy because you have your vision boards plastered all over the place in your home."A vision board is simply a visual representation or collage of the things that you want to have, be, or do in your life. It consists of a poster or foam board with cutout pictures, drawings and/or writing on it of all the things that you want in your life or the things that you want to become. The purpose of a vision board is to activate the law of attraction to begin to pull things from your external environment that will enable you to realize your dream." (selfgrowth.com). By selecting pictures and writing, this charges your emotions with feelings of passion. You will begin to manifest those things into your life. When your direct deposit on Friday steadily increases and you begin to manifest everything that is on your vision board, it will be well worth it. Your friends and peers will begin to take notice, as they will see the increase in lifestyle. They will begin to inquire on what changed.My answer to that is to teach them. Promote what you know and how it can change the lives of others as well, and see the lasting impact that you will have on everyone that you will come in contact with.

I then began to implement G.P.A or Goals Plan Action.I wanted to keep it simple. First, I set goals. You have to have goals, from how much income you want, to as superficial as how many lonely divorced MILFS you want to knock off leaving NIC'S in Beverly Hills on a Friday night. If you are a woman,DILFS. Putting an identifiable number on paper is critical. If you don't have a map, you have no idea where you are going.
Now goals are important, but where the majority of people miss the mark is not having an action list on how you are going to get there. When you set your goals, throw logic out the window.Alexander Graham Bell invented the telephone, and his peers thought he was crazy. Live on the edge a little bit.Write down some goals that when you tell people, they think that you are crazy.Logic is nonexistent when you utilize the powers of your subconscious mind.Having a clear, precise, step-by-step action plan on how you are going to achieve your goal is important. The action is getting off your ass and truly getting after what you want. Have a case of tunnel vision. Focus on your goal to the point where you are consumed by it and go hard or go home. Do not cease until you have achieved your aim.

What separates the 10% from the other 90%? It's the power of the subconscious mind. Any mental road blocks that you might experience, mainly the one mental road block commonly known as "common sense" or "logic," please chuck it. The top 10% have no concept of the term logic. Lodge your logic somewhere else for right now. Let's focus on accomplishing everything that your heart desires. Some of your ambition you might have to keep to yourself. Many people don't want to see you achieve what you have set out to accomplish.

Many people want to rain on your parade or tell you that you can't.I'll give you a prime example: Freshman year in high school, I was forced to run track. I won a couple of races, but when it was time to compete against prime talent – the best of the best – I would get my ass kicked or "butt naked last," as the great sprinter John Drummond would say. Tired of getting embarrassed, I made the decision that I was going to win the state meet by my junior year in the 100 and 200 meters. The head track coach from Vacaville high school told me that "I would not." Me, being up for the challenge, trained my tail off for the next two years. I took what the coach said personal. I trained like a mad man. I had to out-train my competition, and my biggest competitor was me. From 1997-2000, no one in scholastic sports outworked me. Junior year came around, and I ended up leading the nation in the 100-meter dash with a time of 10.50 during the month of April. I did not make it to the state meet that year because of a fluke hamstring injury at a high school football combine weeks before the sub-section meet.

Then comes my senior year. I win the San Joaquin Section title. I had the fastest time in the state in the 100 and 200 10.29 and 21.06 respectfully. At the state meet trials, I ran 10.46, which was the fastest qualifying time in the 100 and 21.18, which was the fastest qualifying time in the 200 for the finals. Finals come around for the 100; the gun blows, I'm in the lead for the first 60 meters then it happens, I blow my hamstring 40 meters short of winning the state meet in the 100. I don't think that it was ever truly meant for me to win state.

Still, during these three years, I learned alot:

#1 – There is no substitute for hard work.

#2 – You have to have a high G.P.A.

Perfect the power of the pen by writing on paper the outcome of what you want to achieve. You have to have tactics to achieve your plan and develop a system that once implemented through action; you become an unstoppable force. Trust me; if I can do it, you can as well. You should expect the best for yourself at all times in life.

Inspire. What does this word conjure up when mentioned? Is it a feeling of euphoria? Or better yet, what inspires you? What makes you get out of bed every day to do what you do? By figuring out what inspires you, this in itself is going to make the G.P.A process a whole lot easier.

4
CHAPTER
A Little Inspiration, Please

When I tell people that I do – sales – the question commonly asked is,"So you go door to door soliciting?" The idea of an individual selling vacuum cleaners is imagined, and the answer is, "Yes, I do go door to door soliciting. I don't consider myself a solicitor; I am too classy to be a solicitor. Soliciting/solicitation has a negative connotation. What inspires me "to solicit"is I know that if I solicit enough, I'll get a sale and by getting the sale, I am now a step closer to purchasing that car or home or whatever my materialistic heart desires. That is what inspires me. You cannot look at work as work. Let me reiterate. You cannot look at work as work.You do not work for your current company; your company works for you. Why? Because your job is affording you the lifestyle that you want to live, also what you learn on your job you can utilize in your personal life or if you have any entrepreneurial interest you can utilize them in your pursuit.

So let's breakdown the word *inspire*. Inspire means"to fill someone with the urge or ability to do or feel something, especially to do something creative,"according to oxforddictionaries.com. To inspire, you need inspiration. The preposition"in"means a position of influence. For example, the "in" crowd "in" expressing movement with the result that someone or something becomes enclosed or surrounded by something else "come in; bring it in,"according to Google dictionary. "Spire" means a tapering conical or pyramidal structure on the top of a building, typically a church tower. So, to be inspired it has to come from the highest point inside of you.

To be inspired, you need some inspiration. Inspiration means "the process of being mentally stimulated to do or feel something. The quality of having been so stimulated,"according to Google dictionary. Here is my favorite definition: "To affect, guide or arouse by divine influence" (from freedictionary.com). Again, if you do not know what inspires you, take the time to find out. This is a major component of G.P.A. Everyone should have something to love, something to do, and something to look forward to. Everyone should be inspired by something meaningful that keeps them anxious at night and ready to be engaged in before their opportunity clock, not alarm clock, goes off, something that keeps you excited every day. Life is miserable without excitement, for it can bemundane and pointless.

If you need something to be inspired about, let's be inspired about making more money. What will an extra 0 at the end of your weekly check do for you? How much money will paying off your car or mortgage free up? At your current job, you could be a promotion away or currently in a position to accomplish all of this.

5

CHAPTER
No Excuses

It could be worse. Trust me; I've been there. You feel as if you are the only one suffering or you are performing the "Why did this happen to me?" song and dance. But remember, *always remember,* to put things in perspective and that it could be worse.

There is a story that a Wiseman, I attract a lot of oracles for some reason, voiced to me. There was a man who complained that he had no shoes, then he walked around the corner, and there was a man sitting without feet; the man without feet complained about obviously having no feet.He then got up, picked up his crutches, crutched around the corner, and there was a man in a wheelchair without legs. No matter what situation you are in, always give thanks, for someone has it worse off than you, and if you don't believe me, go to your nearest homeless shelter.

I live in Los Angeles. There is a section called Skid Row. It has the highest homeless population in America. Think about it in a positive way: L.A. is always sunny, so if you are going to be homeless, you're better off in L.A. I go out there three Sundays out of the month and pass out food. The condition of people on Skid Row is not pleasant. Skid Row is home to the outcast of society or the "least of these,"as said in the Bible. These groups of people have given up on life or are honest people whom have fell on hard times. When I'm out there distributing food, I realize how blessed I am. Like a friend of mine says, "You are too blessed to be stressed, too anointed to be disappointed, and too pigeon-toed to be double-jointed."

Salespeople are truly blessed. We have the opportunity to be in the top 10% of income earners on the planet. We get paid to sell our services/products that are in demand by the general public. Depending on the organization you work for, we pay very low insurance premiums, I have not paid for car insurance in almost three years, and we have at our disposal a list of other perks. Not too many people have the opportunity that we do. So next time you complain about your boss riding your ass because you haven't hit your number, remember: *YOU* control your number. Through hitting your number, you'll be afforded to live the life that you want to live.

Live in a constant state of thanks for you can't be thankful enough. You are truly one lucky individual. Saying thank you over and over is like a form of prayer. Not to get overly religious, but in the Old Testament Book of Genesis, Enoch prayed a 1000 times a day. If you interpret this metaphysically, he said thank you thousands of times each day. In saying thank you, he was blessed.

You are not cold calling; you are walking in the blessings of your life each day. With every knock on the door, be just as thankful when told no as you are told yes because you are even closer to earning the income that you desire. If a woman in a remote Kenyan village can pitch water from a well and walk four miles with the water propped on her head, then you can get off your ass and create some opportunities for you and your family. You have to realize, that it is not only about you. A lot of people are going to benefit from your success. Spread the wealth a little bit and not in a socialistic fashion, but go feed the hungry. Give back and see how you are rewarded.

Enoch walked with God and went to heaven. He was too pure for the planet.

Be in a constant state of thanks, and this will help you in ascending to sales heaven. Sales heaven is a place were setting appointments over the phone and in person isdone effortlessly, everyone wants to buy from you, and more importantly, hefty commissions are always deposited into your account every month.

6

CHAPTER
G.P.A.

If you are the type that says, "Money isn't everything or isn't important," quit lying to yourself. Sales may not be the career path for you, and that's ok. Sales is not for everyone. I'm sorry, but the love of money is not the root of all evil. As long as your intentions are kept pure on what you are going to do with money earned, then the"The love of money is the root of all evil" proverb doesn't apply to you. Get rich – better yet become WEALTHY. Wealth is a measurement of success, and it can be used for good or evil. How it is appropriated is in the hands of the individual who earns it. Just remember to give and to watch your money multiply. Itis a cosmic law.

Don't be discouraged by being told "no," for it's just the law of averages. The more no's that you are told, the closer you are to a sale. Babe Ruth led the MLB in homeruns all-time and homeruns in a year, but he also led the league in strikeouts. Remember, you are doing this for your household. If you dare to quit, you will never realize your potential. Yes, it may be hard at first; yes, you might be overworking yourself and not receiving the due compensation that is reflective of your hard work. Yes, closing only three deals out of 20 new presentations might seem challenging, but through practice, your closing ratio will improve. You have to pay your dues and remember that you are always close to that breakthrough. A caterpillar never realizes that it is destined to become a butterfly. A diamond in its raw uncut state is an inexpensive commodity. It's not until it's polished, that it increases its value by almost a thousand fold.

As long as you have G.P.A. and an unconquerable faith, you can have whatever you want. See everything to the end result; better yet, start at the end result as far as planning goes, and work yourself back to the beginning. By utilizing this technique, you will become excited about living or experiencing the end result through your subconscious mind. Goals are accomplished through energy and excitement. Whatever excites you, utilize it and allow it to manipulate you into the process of manifesting everything that you want. This is the secret of the 10%. In baseball, if you bat .350 or better, you'll go to the hall of fame. If crossword puzzles were easy, no one would do them. If the sales profession were easy, successful salespeople would not get paid the ample commissions that we get paid and that includes you and there would be no presidents club and no all-inclusive trips, for there would be no incentive for your employer to sponsor them. Sales would be just another run-of-the-mill job and the sales force would be comprised of average Joes.

I struggled at the onset of my sales career as well.100% of it was my fault, for I wasn't willing to commit to putting in the extra work that was necessary to be great. I had to swallow a nice ice-cold dose of reality. I realized that A) I was an underachiever and B) walkingaround
with my SEC championship ring like I did when I sold insurance for the duck in Georgia, would not work out here in California. People in California are more concerned with past episodes of *Glee* and if Lindsey Lohan was going back to jail, than a has-been football player walking into their facility with his SEC championship ring on. I was working hard, but I wasn't yielding the fruit of my labor.

Once I made the decision that I wasn't going to be average, I sought out the information that would help improve my skills and become a better sales professional. To be specific, I highly recommend every book by Dale Carnegie. Benchmarking with the top rep in your company is also a good practice. Soon after seeking out the proper help and applying what I learned, sales increased. When sales increase, your income increases, and your personal lifestyle also noticeably becomes better. Overall, you become more of a magnetic and dynamic individual not only in your professional life but also in your personal. When you have a bank account full of money, you are usually more confident and happy. This might not be the case for everyone, but for me, this is what I experienced. Not being overextended financially by bills makes life a little more effortless and pleasant.

7

CHAPTER
Be Assured

Confident salespeople are rarely in a state of anxiety. They rarely panic or feel overwhelmed. Anxiety means that you are in a state of doubt. When you are in a state of doubt, you become stressed. And we all know that pressure breaks pipes. Yes, there are going to be slow days, but slow days need to be turned into sow days. Sow seeds of excitement when you are out in the field. Sow seeds of joy to other people when you are cold calling or walking in the blessings of your life every day. When you walk into the door of any customer, make sure that you at the least make them smile and of course, acquire any relevant information to move the prospect through the sales process. That customer that you just made smile will remember that and maybe one day you will receive an unexpected call from them out of the blue requesting your service. It happens – you have to sow seeds to grow seeds in order to proceed to succeed. To be fruitful you have to plant a seed.

Sowing days are a great opportunity to build your pipeline as well. You have to replenish your pipeline. Do not speak anything negative while you are in a state of sowing. Only speak positive. If you break down the word negative, you have the word *negate* – when in a state of negativity, you negate everything, so stay positive.

The impossible you can turn into the possible. No matter how illogical it might seem for you to get out of your rut, consider it logical. In the Bible,there's the story of Nehemiah who was given the task of rebuilding the wall of Jerusalem. Some said that it would take years to complete, but he rebuilt the wall of Jerusalem in 52 days while being attacked and distracted. The moral of the story is if you are behind your number for the year and there is only one quarter left, it's possible to make up that number. Just know that you have favor in the eyes of GOD and that it can be done. I have seen fellow sales reps who were going into the 4th quarter almost 30%-40% below their sales projection yet hit their number. It's astonishing how people can perform under this type of pressure.

Resist all anxiety. Do not allow anything or anybody to upset you or frustrate you and/or put you in a state of stress. By trusting your process, setting clear definable goalsand having a plan, you know that everything will work in your favor if you just go out into the field every day and give 100%. Many people have lofty and ambitious goals, many people have a plan, but only a few get out of bed day in and day out and produce. It's called W.O.W. – Works Over Words.

Always assume the sale. How do you assume the sale one might ask? Being an expert in your prospective clients' field is one. Knowing as much information as possible about your prospective client,personal and professional, before you meet is another. Once you are in front of your prospect, set the agenda. Your prospect needs to know that this appointment wasn't set so that you all can make friends; you want them to buy your service/product as well. Having three prepared questions that can open up dialogue to find out buying motives and why they agreed to schedule the appointment is important as well. An example is"What separates you from your competitors?""Whom is your favorite vendor and why?""Do you plan on expanding?" By following these steps, you will feel more confident. Your confidence will radiate to the point that every potential buyer that you come across will notice it, which will increase your chances to make the sale. Everyone wants to deal with someone that has swagger and whom is an expert in his/her field.

8

CHAPTER
Tell Your SalesJourney

Keep a journal in which you tell your sales journey. Everything that happens throughout the day of your daily sales career, you should put on paper and into a specific book/journal. Telling your sales journey is important in pinpointing buying tendencies. For example,an excerpt in my journal mentioned not to offer industrial-looking dispensers in the high-end restrooms of Beverly Hills restaurants. Every time that I do,I'm confronted with a look of confusion from usually the GM of the restaurant on why I would even consider offering a big piece of plastic to hang up in their stainless steel and marble restrooms. These GMs at times feel insulted. Document everything so that you can refer back to it. Always write a brief reflection about your day, from what you wore, to what you ate. Document it all – what type of industry you called on that day, what products and services are hot right now. Note your successes and "failures" throughout your career.

Journaling serves as a great tool for reminiscing on your sales career from its inception. Sales journals are a great memoir. Back in the day when I was in 100% commission – only sales with absolutely no perks (such as very content with this type of existence, for I did not know the science of the subconscious mind yet. I became complacent. Instead of getting off my ass and cold calling, I would sleep in to 9a.m., get up,and check my backstage page, because I was an aspiring actor at the time. I would start doing some insurance work briefly such as maybe make a phone call or two, and then get dressed. I was out the door at noon. Noon, you know what that means – lunch time. I would find the nearest Mexican restaurant,for I am a Mexican food aficionado, order five carne asada tacos, finish lunch around two, hop back in my car and drive around office parks for an hour, and have every excuse on why I should not get out of the car. By 3:30, I'd get out of the car onsite at maybe five businesses and get their cards. By 4:25 it was gym time because if I waited to five, all the equipment would be in use so I had to beat the after-work gym rush.

Here is a sales vitamin: You need to be shaking a decision maker's hand no later than 9a.m. every morning.The reason why I was on this laxschedule was because I received a BIG commit from a "target" account. In salesman terms, an account that was going to yield a huge commission check and we sales people get paid on commits. YEAH RIGHT. Also, this account would have placed me at quota for the year. Well, the commit reneged, and I was in deep financial trouble. By the grace of God, one early cold December day, my manager calls me and tells me, "That there is a massive account in Tennessee that he needed my help signing up and he would split the commission with me." If it wasn't for that, I would have been in the poor house literally – probably someone's soup kitchen – but once again, prayers answered and another safety net was there to save me.

9

CHAPTER
Getting What You Want

If you see something you want, by all means possess it, don't live on pins and needles. With sales,well with any decent sales company, you will have the opportunity to earn uncapped commissions. So your earning potential is limitless. With that being said, if you want the 750 BMW, by all means go and buy it. Rolex watch?Go get it.If you work a proper plan, a little GPA, you will have more than enough to buy,depending on your tastes, the majority of the materialistic items that your heart desires and save a boatload of money.

A lot of people forget to do this, but you should be a blessing in other people's lives. You will have enough money to give and to give substantially. Every time I have had an increase in expenses, I have found a way to earn more money and to give more.Materialistic items are placed here on this earth to enjoy. It was meant for you tocruise on the 405 in your newly bought Porsche 911. Enjoy the bounty and spoils that you have earned throughout your sales career, and remember to practice the art of philanthropy to ensure that you "Pay It Forward."

Higher consciousness will always see and make sure that you are spoiled. Yes, I said it "spoiled." Your grandparents spoiled you whenever they had the opportunity, so the most high wants to spoil you as well. It's funny, a lot of people can be overly cautious when it comes to their lifestyle. I was so ready to get out of my PT Cruiser that when I was presented with opportunity to get my first luxury vehicle – a Porsche Cayenne S, which I affectionately named "Ebony", people advised me not to get it, because of maintenance cost and God forbid the "What if you get fired or lose your job?"Warning: The fear mongering I didn't resonate on. So, I bought the Porsche. Yes, I have had some small mechanical issues as with any car, but the feeling that you get when you get in and out of a vehicle that makes you excited and also serves as a testimony to the fruit that you reap through your efforts is priceless. Side note: Fellas, please do not ever buy a PT Cruiser or Nissan Cube or any car in that family. If you do mind being the butt of every joke or people giving you weird looks, or picking up a girl and taking her out on her first date in it then wondering why she has not called you back, don't do it. Stay clear away from them. You will lose so many cool points and will not have any swagger.

In life, you should not settle. You should only satisfy People, get what you want – go and buy it now, but please refrain from being reckless. Meaning, don't go blow your entire life savings and your kid's college funds on a phantom, and please do not purchase a phantom while you are still renting a studio apartment in Koreatown. Purchasing one will be a terrible use of judgment on your behalf. Be reasonable and utilize Sound Right Reasoning in all aspects of your life.
Remember, safe is the new risky. Don't play life so safe. If you want a safe life, quit sales and go get a government job. That is about as safe as you can get, from what I understand.

You have to ask yourself, "Why Do I do sales?" There are a number of other professions. Sales is not a safe career. Trust me, it's only safe when you are performing at a high-caliber level. Again, if you trust your process, ensuring that your process is a method that enables you to be successful in the time of so called slowness, you will be fine. You will be protected by safety net after safety net. Why a career in sales? Because it affords you the opportunity to realize your potential and maximize your talents.Salesis one of the only professions where you will have to perform at a high-caliber level at all times – and if you don't, your pay will take a plunge.

10

CHAPTER
You Have To PlayHurt

Y ou have to play hurt. Shit is going to happen to disrupt your day. Again, if sales was easy, everyone would want to do it. If you wake up with a runny nose, wipe your nose, take some Dayquil, and get out there and sell. Expect the unexpected when you are out in the field. I swear, every four months I have an issue with my car, lol – i.e., accidents, vandalized, something breaking down, etc. When that happens, I get it towed, get a rental, and get back out to the field and sell. Every minute not in the field is a lost opportunity to close a deal. Don't be distracted while you are out in the field. If your nagging, gossiping mother-in-law calls you, press ignore and keep pushing. If your first two appointments cancel for the day, go cold call and make something happen. If the department manager is threatening to write you up because you're not hitting your quota, you control that. Revise your plan or lack thereof and make something happen.

And when situations like the ones stated above take place, just laugh at them. Laughter is the best weapon against anything adverse. Keep the humor in it. What I do whenever I am having a "bad" day, I become a kid again.(We will assume that the majority of kids never have a worry in the world). I listen to the music of my childhood, i.e. The Jets,New Edition, and The Boys.It takes me back in time to when I was a child and didn't have to worry about anything. If any adverse situations come my way, I don't worry about them for it will workout in my favor.

Go and give randomly. Feed someone on the streets or go volunteer. It puts everything back in perspective. People are going through worse than you. The giving of gifts exhausts the ego. Whenever we are complaining about how things aren't going our way, or you can't get that break, or how everything on the planet is conspiring against you, it's just your ego talking. Suppress it.

Be relentless, and in being relentless if you make a mistake that is fine. Why do they put erasers on pencils?Erasers give you the opportunity to correct your mistakes. It is a metaphor for life as well. We all make mistakes. If someone tells you that they are perfect, slap them because they are lying. But in making your mistakes/failures, be firm in your resolve, hold your position if only that you truly know that your process is going to place you on a path to success. Again, everyone is going to experience failure; how you respond to the adversity of failure is going to determine your success. Hold your position. It's ok at times to make a mistake because it affords you the opportunity to correct it in the future. As Malcolm X said, "Every defeat, every heartbreak, every loss, contains its own seed, its own lesson on how to improve your performance next time."

11

CHAPTER
The Salesman Diet/Nice Guys
Finish 1st

Go into your sales presentation hungry. Do not over indulge in Chinese and Indian buffets at lunch. Ok, I am going to confess that at times I am greedy and delight at the local Los Angeles Indian buffets. When it comes to food, I can be gluttonous, but please do not follow my example. If after lunch you have the *itis*– "slang for ready to take a nap because all of your blood is rushing to your stomach because you pigged out and ate too much."– during your sales presentations, you will not have the energy to be the charismatic and dynamic individual that you are. Presenting is equal to going into a championship game or tennis match or any other athletic competition where the outcome decides the victor. Ray Lewis isn't going to eat three platefuls of chicken masala and rice pudding before his playoff game against the Colts. He would not perform at an optimal level. Instead of all of the blood and oxygen flowing to his muscles and organs that he needs to utilize the most during play, the blood and oxygen is going to concentrate on his gut, which will lead to tummy aches and time spent in the lockerroom on the toilet during the game. Trust me, I've been there. So, if all of your energy is being focused on digesting all of the General Tso chicken that you just recently devoured, that is energy that is not going into your presentation.

Maintain high energy at all times. Eat light. I usually drink a fruit smoothie for breakfast, or what I call "breaking the fast" of your sleep and then for lunch, a tuna sandwich, bag of Sun Chips, fruit and desert. I'm addicted to Subway Oatmeal raisin cookies and Quiznos snicker doodle cookies; these are by far the best cookies on the planet. Talk to any athlete that was worth a damn and ask them their pre-game diets. They ate very light. An ideal pre-game meal for me, when I ran track and played football,was a bowl of oatmeal and fruit. Last thing you want is to be in the starting blocks with an upset stomach.

Psychologically, eating light causes you to be hungry, which causes you to go into your sales presentations hungry and wanting the deal even more. Just like my football coach use to voice, "Go into your athletic competitions hungry." Everything is connected and everything is related. Eat light, go into your sales presentations hungry, and allow the energy to flow to your body language and not your full gut. While you are in your sales presentation hungry, you will have the hunger for more, hunger for more presentations, which will equate to more sales. At the end of a successful sales day, go and pig out. Enjoy your post-game meal. You deserve it.

Make sure you are drinking plenty of water while out in the field, about a gallon a day.Water is life.Just like the planet, 70% of the human body is made up of water. Drink plenty of water and stay balanced and one with Mother Nature. All of your sales calls/presentations will flow more naturally.Utilize the following hydration test to determine if you are hydrated or not: When you urinate, if it is not clear, you are not fully hydrated and therefore need todrink more water. The yellower, the more dehydrated you are. No, I'm not going to watch you urinate, but I will be sending a memo to all sales managers to watch each individual on their sales force urinate to ensure that their urine is clear. Let's see if HR approves.It's important to know the correlation between proper hydration and sales.

I had a football coach in college who in his Monday afternoon meetings would stress how if we would cease smokingand drinking on Thursdays – 48 hours before game day – how much on a higher level we would compete on Saturdays.Just a change like this can be the difference between having the awareness and speed to grab a pick or to give up a quick six. Translation: Have a good time on the weekend, but don't get hammered to the point where it would affect your Monday performance at work. If you are not able to work at an optimal level on Monday because you got blasted on Sunday, you now are left with four days in the selling week instead of five. Again, you owe it to yourself to be in a position to perform at your max while on the clock.

The majority of the top athletes on the planet are the nicest guys/gals off of the field; yes, there mightbea few ass-holes, but for the most part, they are all approachable. Be well mannered while in the field, in life, in general. In the field, you have to be passive-aggressive, meaning if told "no," always keep a smile on your face and in your heart while handling the objection. After all,"It's nice to be important, but it's more important to be nice."

Always be in a state of peace, but use business as a platform to exercise your aggression. Get out there and compete. Some people say you don't have to compete as long as you create…I consider that a half-truth. You will always be competing. Since the dawn of man, there has been competition. Look at the Forbes Top 500 list – everyone wants to be #1. If a company does not want the recognized as #1 on the Forbes 500 list, they sound like the sales rep that tells you that money isn't everything. Money/ profitability *is* the measurement of success in the business world. Yes, you might have a niche market.You might be the first in a certain field offering a unique service or product, but someone soon will be coming along offering a similar service or product that claims to be more revolutionary or better than yours…Here comes the competition. What are you going to do to separate yourself from the pack? Success is measured in numbers. First place is first to win; second place is the first to lose.

You have to compete.Get that spiritual notion out of your head that there is no competition just creation. There is a little bit of both. If you want to be the top sales rep, then create and be different in the way that you are offering your service. This will separate you from your peers, but your boss/upline is still going to be measuring you by where do you rank in your sales force and how much you have sold. Me personally, I love to compete. I love winning all of the sales contests. If you have a heartbeat and if you are in sales, competition should play a role in you wanting to be successful. Who doesn't want their name in lights? What company doesn't want to be #1 in their industry?

If you are not up to it, I would recommend venturing to Tibet and sitting in the lotus position or starting a 501c3 nonprofit. Allow me to retract that statement, seeing the tactics of nonprofits here in L.A., they are more aggressive at times in soliciting for donations in front of Trader Joes on Vine Street in Hollyweird than I am going door to door.

Fellow sales people, always have the competitive mindset. Challenge yourself.Set your expectations higher than normal. Go above and beyond. I have utilized this technique often. At the onset, when you tell your peers that you are going to sale some obscene amount for the quarter/year, they might look at you crazy. Once you have achieved it, not only do you change your mindset, your peers change their mindset as well. You have now raised the expectations for yourself and the people around you. No more just settling for average or doing just enough to get by so you don't get fired. Roger Bannister told everyone that he was going to break the four-minute mile. He trained like a madman, and people thought he was crazy. Well, he broke the four-minute mile; something that people thought would be impossible. Shortly thereafter, people started to break the four-minute mile with ease. So, set a new standard be an innovator.

Always be receptive, and treat everyone with the same respect that you would want to be treated with. I know that in sales our time is valuable, and in most cases, we are making more money than the business owner that we are pitching to buy our service and products. Even if you do not sell the product or service try to get something out of the person. It does not always have to be monetary. I swear that some of my most memorable moments from when I was in the field are from people that did not buy from me or have not even bought from me yet. Sometimes it's just bad timing. They are not ready, or they just do not have the money at the moment. At times, I will be given a life jewel from this individual that can help me along my personal journey.

Raphael at Berris on Third Street here in L.A. is a great example. He has not purchased any of my services yet, but he has shared some valuable life lessons with me. One is the book *The Alchemist,* a story of a young man who is in search for a treasure. He does not find the treasure, but the experiences that he has gained while on this search is the treasure are invaluable.

Or take Shadi at Calumet Photo in L.A.:"First place is first to win; second place is first to lose." Very Ricky Bobbish, but in reality, it is the truth.

I know at times that it can be a lonely journey and that we can get beat up by the elements in our sales universe. Customers might beat us up, so in return, we can at times become very abrasive and impatient with prospects whom are genuinely interested but cannot express this interest properly. Still, give them a high level of respect and just have a general conversation with them. Build a ton of rapport, and by just being a dynamic and nice individual, you will experience a plethora of good karma that is coming your way. Always smile inside and out. A.B.S – Always Be Smiling in whatever you do and see what you attract. Make it your business to learn from every prospect one unique thing that can benefit you. Even if you did not end up with the contract, you can still learn something. When prospects vent on how the economy is slow, which in turn is causing their business to slow down, give them words of encouragement.

At times prospects will want you to be miserable like them. Often questions/statements like "My business is slow and businesses in the area are slow. Everyone is struggling around here; how is business for you?" This is a trap question. As they say, "Misery enjoys company." You answer, "Awesome," even if it is not. Do not partake in the "let'sfeel sorry for each other" chatter, but be a listening ear and give sound advice. Now I understand that we do not get paid to be therapists, but sometimes asimple good gesture can go a long way.

12

CHAPTER
Acres of Diamonds

Opportunity is everywhere, there is and always will be an acre of diamonds in your territory. Your job is to uncover and dig up these diamonds.

A common complaint from sales reps is the myth that their territory has been exhausted, that they've knocked on every door, and there aren't any more opportunities, people aren't just buying,etc. This is not the case. Do not accept these myths as reality. If a customer says "no," continue to go back to that customer. What occurs often in L.A., is changes in personnel. People get fired. People get promoted, and with that being said, the new hire might have a different way in handling their business. They might see the benefit in utilizing your services. They might have used you in the past at a different location and want to implement your program. If the same contact that told you "no" the first time is still there,keep going back but don't be a nuisance. Be "Passive Aggressive." Know the fine line between being persistent and being annoying. As Tywan Freeney, a friend in Atlanta who owns Dream 21 personal training studios once told me,"Persistence beats resistance."

Where you are right now, you are standing on acres of diamonds, waiting to be mined. Therearediamond mines under your feet that are waiting to be extracted, cut, polished and then distributed. Right now, as we speak, opportunity is everywhere. If you have not read or heard the "Acre of Diamonds" story, look it up and read it. It talks about an individual who leaves his farm in search for opportunity – the business opportunity is in harvesting diamonds. He sells his farm. He goes on his search, doesn't find anything, goes crazy, and drowns himself in a river. The new owner of the farm discovers diamonds under this farm and strikes it rich. The moral of the story is opportunity/success is closer than you think.

As long as you can do better than someone in a particular field, compete and be unique, you have an opportunity to be successful. No one or nothing holds the key to your advancement. You are always closer than you think. You should always live where you want to live. You shouldn't have to be miserable in a city that you don't want to live in because of the "opportunity." I repeat, opportunity is everywhere. Remember, if it is truly yours it will come to you. You don't have to go to it. It's called the law of least resistance – once you stop reaching for it, it will come to you. No matter how long it takes, you are going to keep pressing forward and your goal will be reached. Don't allow your current circumstances to force you to abandon your plan. Through the decisions that you make, you control your own destiny.

13
CHAPTER
You're in Control

Be responsible. We are responsible for the outcome of all of our actions. What we put in is what we put out. Be responsible for your vision. If you are not satisfied with the outcome of something, you be responsible and cause the change. For every cause, there is an effect. You can either be the effect of the cause or cause of the effect. Be the director of your movie, for you choose the cast you write the plot and you decide the outcome. Yes, you are responsible to attain the outcome that you desire. Even though you are responsible for the outcome, you will still have twist and turns and surprises in your story. Who watches a movie where every single scene is predictable? It doesn't make for a good movie. So don't get discouraged, and don't show any forms of distress. You are still in control. You still have to be responsible.

If anything unexpected is thrown at you, respond in a fashionable manner. In responding in a fashionable manner, you respond in an elegant and effortless manner. Make it look easy. Be as smooth as possible; that is, be a smooth operator.

Here we go, another sports analogy. Joe Montana, in my opinion, is the greatest quarterback of all time. When it came to fourth quarter comeback heroics,he was Mr. Cool. Take the 1989 Super Bowl against the Cincinnati Bengals for example. The San Francisco 49ers were down by three points with 3:20 left when Montana spotted not an open receiver but a personality. "There, in the stands, standing near the exit ramp," Montana said to tackle Harris Barton, "Isn't that John Candy?" He then led the 49ers 92 yards throwing for the winning touchdown with 34 seconds left. Now, Montana was not the prototypical 6'5 230-pound strong-arm quarterback; he was just one of the guys that was born to be a quarterback. So are you.

You are born and wired to be a successful salesperson. If you weren't, you wouldn't be in the position that you are in today. All is mental and you have the mental fortitude and aptitude to cause whatever outcome you desire. The masses of people are carried along obedient to their environment, to the wills and desires of others stronger than themselves, to heredity, to suggestions, and to other outbound causes moving them about like fish on the hook of life. But the masters rise to the place above, dominate their moods, characters, qualities and powers, as well as the environment surrounding them, and become fishers of men instead of fish. They help to play the game of life instead of being played and moved about by other wills and environment. They use the principle instead of being its tools. The masters are responsible. They use trials as an opportunity to do things differently.

Whenever I experience a trial, I learn something new. I am forced to find a new route or take a detour to success. If my athletic career wasn't taken from me, I wouldn't be writing this book right now. I probably wouldn't be the philanthropist that I am right now, and I probably wouldn't have been interested in traveling to Africa and climbing Mt. Kilimanjaro. I wouldn't be as cultured. During my jock days, all I thought about and all I could breathe, eat, and sleep was girls, track/football and money. This lifestyle would have led me down a path to self-destruction. More than likely, I would be broke right now, for I was not the most responsible with finances.

People wonder how a millionaire can go broke. It's very easy. First of all, the majority of people who claim to be millionaires are not millionaires. If you get an upfront signing bonus of $1,000,000 after Uncle Sam pulls both of his fist out of your ass you are left with around maybe $650,000if you have a decent accountant. Then of course, your expenses are going to be high. You then have to take care of the other leeches that want a part of you – family members and friends with their hands out, etc. Usually, a lifestyle like this is not sustainable. You get cut and then you have to figure out how to make a living for yourself that can keep up with your current lifestyle and spending habits. So consciousness or God or whatever you want to call it had a different plan. He put an end to my professional sports inspirations. Random thought: It's ok to tell family and friends, no matter what they have claimed to have done for you in the past, NO. Those who have unconditional love,what your friends and or family might have claimed that they have for you, won't throw in your face instances of how they helped you in the past and use that to manipulate you into forcing you to help them. Love doesn't do that, plus you have the right to disagree or say no as well. Your family and friends might need to get off their ass and cold call as well – this just isn't exclusively for sales people.

Sometimes we do not understand the plan of the most high. God's plan might not reveal itself to us immediately. As in the story of Musa/Moses and Al Khidr, who is also known as Melchizedek in the Bible, the following story is taken from The Quran. Musa on his search for knowledge and understanding finally seeks out the most mysterious man in the Quran/Bible, Al Khidr, who has no parents or no beginning or end. He is also nicknamed the tester, and from reading this story you will grow to understand why. The prophet Musa greeted Al-Khidr and asked him,"May I follow you so that you teach me of that knowledge you have been taught?" Al Khidr

43

replied,"Verily you will not be able to remain patient with me." Musa becomes insistent and says,"You will find me, in case Allah (so) decides, patient; and I will not disobey you in any command (of yours)" So Al Khidr obliges and allows Musa to set off on a journey with him. "So they both went off until, when they embarked in the ship, Al Khidr pierced it. Musa said, "Have you pierced it so as to drown its population (i.e., passengers). "Al Khidr said, "Did I not say that surely you would never be able to endure with me patiently?"Musa responded,"Do not take me to task that I forgot, nor oppress me with a command too difficult for me." (TMQ 18:71-73)

So then after their first journey, Al Khidr andMusaembarked on their second journey:"So they both went off until when they both met a youth, then he killed him. He said, 'Have you killed a most cleansed self without(his having killed another) Self? Indeed, you have already come with a (highly) maleficent thing." Said he, 'Did I not say to you that surely you would never be able to endure with me patiently?" He said, "In case I ask you about anything after (this), then keep me in (your) company (no more) you have already had (literally revealed) excuse (sufficient) on my part." (literally; from close me)" (TMQ 18:74-76).

Off again they went on their third journey. "So they both went off until, when they came up to the population of a city, they asked its population for food, yet they refused to receive them as guests. Then they found therein a wall that would have collapsed down, so he set it up. He said, 'If you so decided, indeed you could have taken to yourself a reward for it.'" Al Khidr responds, "This is the parting between me and you. I will soon(fully) inform you regarding the interpretation of what you were unable to endure patiently.

"As for the ship, then it belonged to certain persons who did their business upon the sea. Then I willingly damaged it, and beyond them was a king who was taking away every ship by force."

There was an evil king whom lived in a village nearby whom was seizing ships. The king would not seize any ships that were damaged, that is why Al Khidr damaged the ship that he was aboard for he knew what laid ahead; the ship was of economic value to the village so the village could not lose it to the tyrant king.

Of journey #2, the Quran says, "And as for the youth, then his parents were believers; so we were apprehensive he would oppress them with (his) in ordinance and disbelief. (TMQ,18:80)So we willingly (intended) that their Lord would give them (both) in exchange a more charitable (person) in cleansing (i.e. a better, purer son) than he a nearer in tenderness" (TMQ 18:81).

The most high knew that the future of this boy was that he would become a tyrant.If this boy had lived, he would have been destined to be an oppressor. His death was beneficial to the society, to his parents and himself.

Final, he tells about journey #3. "And for the wall, then it belonged to two orphan youths in the city and beneath it was a hoarding belonging to them, and their father was a righteous man. So your Lord willed that they should reach full age and take out their hoarding as a mercy from your lord, and in no way did I perform it upon my own command. This is the interpretation of what you were unable to endure patiently."

The father of the two orphans knew that the villagers were very miserly, so he hid the treasure under the wall until they were strong

45

enough to unearth it. When Al Khidr passed by the wall, he saw that it was about to fall, and so he fixed the wall to ensure that the treasure would remain safe until the orphans reached maturity (Abdurrahman.-org).

My original intention was not to write out all three journeys in detail, but to just focus on one and with that, the moral of the story would be received. Instead, I went into detail about all three journeys because of how like Musa,"Moses", situations that are presented to us can seem unclear and confusing. They may not work in our favor at first, but with higher consciousness, everything – no matter how much failure has been presented to us – works out for our good. Be patient and still work your process, no matter what. Success will present itself no matter what contradicting setting we are presented with.

No matter how many books you read, no matter how many affirmations you may recite, you will be tested to make sure that you are steadfast in your consciousness. And trust me, being steadfast in your consciousness, system or whatever you want to call it, you surely will be rewarded as long as you hold your position while in a season of calamity. You have to be presented with loss to appreciate and truly understand the definition of victory.

14

CHAPTER
Developing Your Mental Muscles

What makes you strong? If you do not know now, trust me, in times of adversity you will find out. Knowing these traits will help you in the long run.

Another good question to ask yourself is what are you afraid of? By answering this question, you can now identify fears, isolate them and figure out a strategy to overcome them and attack them head-on or just replace them with something positive.

Times of struggle also afford you with the opportunity to reflect and put things into perspective. Writing this book serves as a method of reflection for me. Currently, I am having a "slow" quarter – remember, we don't say slow, we say sow, because the seeds that you sow when you get off of your ass and cold call, will grow into a Touba tree. The Touba tree is the tree of paradise. Charles Dickens transmuted his pain/suffering through novels that are read till this day worldwide. Jean-Michel Basquiat's art reflected his inner battles.

The lyrics of Tupac Shakur's music tell of the struggle that he faced. Here is one of my favorite poems from his book of poetry, *The Rose That Grew from Concrete*: "Did you hear about the rose that grew from a crack in the concrete? Proving nature's love is wrong; it learned to walk without having feet. Funny it seems, but by keeping its dreams, it learned to breathe fresh air. Long live the rose that grew from concrete when no one else ever cared."

15
CHAPTER
Get Out And Cold Call

Cold calling is still an effective sales tactic if done right. The obituary for cold calling is premature. While in the perfect world your phone would be ringing off the hook all day with clients offering you business, the reality is that if you want business, you need to go after it, and cold calling is an effective sales tactic if it's done properly. Here are some structured cold calling tips.

1) Focus on the goal.
Beginners tend to think that cold calling is about making the sale. It's not. It's about getting the chance to make the sale. Specifically, the purpose of a cold call is to set an appointment to make the pitch.

2) Research your markets and prospects.
You need to target your cold calling to the right audience. Use market research to focus on your target market. Then find out as much as youpossibly can about the company or individual you're going to call in advance. This gives you the huge advantage of being able to talk about their business and their needs when you call them.

3) Prepare an opening statement for your call.
This lets you organizeyour thoughtsbeforecalling, and
helps you avoid common mistakes in the opening that would give the person you're calling the chance to terminate the conversation. For instance, you should never ask, "Is this a good time to talk?" or "How are you today?" Don't read your opening statement into the phone,

but use it as a framework to get the cold calling conversation off to a good start.

4) What should be in the opening statement?

This organizational scheme for cold calling (All Business.com) works well: "Include a greeting and an introduction, a reference point (something about the prospect), the benefits of your product or service, and a transition to a question or dialogue. For example, 'Good afternoon, Ms. Marshall. This is Ken Brown with Green Works. I read in the local paper that you recently broke ground for a new office complex. We specialize in commercial landscape services that allow you to reduce in-house maintenance costs and comply with the city's new environmental regulations. I'd like to ask a few questions to determine whether one of our programs might meet your needs.'"

5) Prepare a script for the rest of your call.

Lay out the benefits of your product or service and the reasons your prospect should buy. Write out possible objections and your answer to them. Without a cold calling script, it's too easy to leave something out or to meander. You won't be reading your script word for word when you call but have prepared the framework of the cold call in advance.

6) Ask for an appointment at a specific time.

Say, "Would Wednesday at 11 a.m. be a good time to meet?" instead of saying, "Can I meet with you to discuss this next week?"

7) Remember that gatekeepers are your allies not your foes.

Be pleasant to whoever picks up the phone or is guarding the inner sanctum when cold calling. Develop strategies to get the gatekeeper on your side. Sometimes asking, "I wonder if you could help me?" will help you get the information you need, such as the name of the right person to talk to or when the best time to contact the prospect is. Learning the names of gatekeepers and being friendly when cold calling helps, too.

8) Smooth the way for your call by sending prospects a small, unique promotional item.
This helps break the ice and makes your business stand out from thecrowd. Pat Cavanaugh, sales guru of Inc.com, says, "It's amazing. A \$2.15 crazy little item we've sent out has helped us get Fortune 500 accounts. When we call, they say, 'You were the one that sent me that...'"

9) Do your cold calling early in the morning, if possible.
That's the best time to reach the decision-maker directly and for most people the time that they're most energized.

10) Be persistent.
"Eighty percent of new sales are made after the fifth contact, yet the majority of sales people give up after the second call" (AllBusiness.com).And above all, practice, practice, practice. While cold calling may never be much fun for you, you can get better at it, and the more you practice, the more effective a sales tactic it will be. So get your script and your call list together and reach for the phone. The people who want to do business with you are out there – but you have to let them know about you first.

"If the thought of cold calling makes your stomach drop to your toes, these tips won't eliminate your fear, but they will help you make cold calling a more successful experience." (sbinfocanada)

CLOSING

At times, cold calling can have a negative connotation amongst us sales professionals and people in general. But in reality, you are not cold calling, you are walking in the blessings of your life each and every day. Through every door that you knock on, you are afforded an opportunity to not only to improve your personal lifestyle but also the lifestyle of those that you are responsible for. You are truly in control of your destiny and the destiny of the ones you love when cold calling. I want to share a poem with you by William Ernest Henley that correlates with cold calling and destiny; it's called *Invictus*:

Out of the night that covers me,
Black as the Pit from pole to pole,
I thank whatever gods may be
For my unconquerable soul.

In the fell clutch of circumstance
I have not winced nor cried aloud.
Under the bludgeonings of chance
My head is bloody but unbowed.

Beyond this place of wrath and tears
Looms but the Horror of the shade,
And yet the menace of the years
Finds, and shall find, me unafraid.
It matters not how strait the gate,
How charged with punishments the scroll.
I am the master of my fate:
I am the captain of my soul.

So at the end of the day, which is the beginning of the moment, which is right now, **GET OFF YOUR ASS AND COLD CALL!!!**

ABOUT THE AUTHOR

Dynast Amir,full name Dynast Abefe Adewale Amir, is a dynamic, globetrotting, entrepreneur and philanthropist,who has a passion for life and seeing the success of others. Dynast was born Albert Horton Hollis II in Sacramento,CA, but considers himself a displaced African who just happened to be born in America. He attended Christian Brothers High School in Sacramento, where he would star in track and football earning 1st team Parade and USA Today High School All-American honors in football. After graduating from Christian Brothers, he would then take his talents to the University of Georgia. He would letter in track and football and graduate with a degree in Agricultural Business. After a short stint in modeling and acting, he would take his talents to Corporate America.Dynast would finish in the top 10% in sales for two fortune 500 companies organizations, Aflac and Cintas. This culminated with him finishing #1 in the entire sales organization at Cintas Corporation in 2014.In 2018, Dynast would leave Corporate America to take his talents to Africa to focus full time on implementing several much needed initiatives geared towards improving infrastructure on many levelsas well as bridging the gap between the diaspora and Africa.Dynast currently serves as the Omo Oba, Prince in Yoruba, of Ororuwo, Nigeria and encourages everyone to come and visit the Kingdom of Ororuwo."Sales is the greatest opportunity for any young professional out of college to earn a considerable amount of income in a short period of time."– Dynast Amir

Made in the USA
Middletown, DE
27 September 2020